To

D0324361

From

To a very special®
DAUGHTER

Illustrations by Juliette Clarke.
Written by Pam Brown.
Edited by Helen Exley.

HELEN EXLEY®

Other books in the TO-GIVE-AND-TO-KEEP™ series:
To a very special FRIEND   To my very special LOVE
To a very special MOTHER   To a very special GRANDMOTHER
To a very special HUSBAND   To my very special WIFE

Published in 1991 by Helen Exley Giftbooks in Great Britain.
This edition published in 2008

12   11   10   9   8   7   6   5   4

ISBN 13: 978-1-84634-205-9

Illustrations by Juliette Clarke. Written by Pam Brown. Edited by Helen Exley.
Important Copyright Notice: PAM BROWN © HELEN EXLEY 1991, 2008
Printed in China.
'TO A VERY SPECIAL'® IS A REGISTERED TRADE MARK OF HELEN EXLEY GIFTBOOKS

Helen Exley Giftbooks, 16 Chalk Hill, Watford, Herts WD19 4BG, UK.
www.helenexleygiftbooks.com

I often wondered before you came...
Did I want a frilly daughter or a chunky,
cheerful child? Did I want her to be
an administrator? Or caring? Or both?
As it was, I didn't get any of my dreams.
I got a totally unique, totally new, totally
puzzling, unpredictable, delightful you.

I keep an album of photographs of you – as if
I could hold on to all the different yous –
the baby, the toddler, the schoolgirl,
the teenager. But they don't really matter.
Not that much. Because you are all of them
– and every time I see you I think,
"This is the best time."

Dear daughter. I think of you *all* the time.
When I find the dye from your
T-shirt has patterned most things in the wash.
When I find long hairs in the drain pipe.
When I'm scrubbing the bath oil scum
off the bath. When I find a half-eaten bar
of chocolate in your bed. When I discover
you've consumed *all* the ice-cream,
just before dinner. When I find a yoghurt pot
full of primroses by my bed.
I love you.

Thanks for all the cards – hand drawn
or by Monet. For all the parcels
– knobbly or beribboned.
For all the hurried kisses
– smelling of chocolate or Chanel.
For remembering.

Sometimes I wish I had the power to make things
come right for you. Sometimes I wish I had
money enough to give you the things
you dream of. Sometimes I wish I had treasures
to pass on to you. But I gave what I could
– your five bright senses, the world about you.
Take what you want, add your own wonder
to the sum of all human wonder, and pass on
the gift of love. It is enough.

Dear daughter. I wish you eyes to see
– the gull's gawkish walk, the turn of leaves,
the coil of running water, the spurt of raindrops
on a shining street,

rainbows, a swirl of starlings in a city sky.
I wish you ears to hear –
the murmur of hidden streams, a morning robin,
scufflings in the hedgerow,
the sound of traffic muted by summer trees,
anchor cable running out,
the hush of voices as the curtain rises.
Smells haunting and sharp, enticing, evanescent.
The first violets, clean linen, roast chestnuts.
The touch of silk and sun-warmed stone.
Cats. And familiar, loving hands.
The taste of new bread, of clear water,
of the *vin du pays*, of a newly-picked tomato.
Dear daughter – I wish you life.

Daughters are given to making announcements.
I'm joining an ashram. I've signed on to crew
a boat to Singapore. I've invited my headteacher
to dinner... Today. I'm getting a tattoo.
I'm leaving home. I'm going to be a nun.
I'm moving back home. I'm having my hair
dyed pink. I'm going to settle down just as soon
as I've sailed around the Horn.

Having daughters is the best investment
you will ever make against becoming bored.

Life since you came has been like an
extraordinary book – one where I just can't
wait to turn the page and see what new thing
you have done. I don't know which I like best –
the quiet chapters – or the big dramatic scenes
– or the cliff-hangers. It's never dull.
I just can't get over the fact that I had a hand
in the authorship.

IN PRAISE

I'm proud of all your achievements.
You've worked hard for them. I'm proud
of your looks and your intelligence –
which some far distant ancestor
handed down. But I'm most proud of your
being just *you*. "Success" would be an extra
– but you are special to me *whatever* you do.

I'm proud of you not for the things
that came easily to you – or that were part
of you from the very beginning – but for
your slogging it out against the odds
and against your nature and spluttering
to the surface with your prize.

No. You are not perfect – and I am sorry
that when you were small I sometimes seemed
to demand perfection. You are better
than perfect. You are a unique piece of humanity,
fallible, questing, always astonishing in your
discoveries and dreams. I am everlastingly
thankful that a little of me is caught up
in your being, and that you carry me into
a future that I shall never know.
You are all of us – and yet yourself forever.

In a world where it is necessary to succeed,
perhaps only we women know more deeply
that success can be a quiet and hidden thing.

Dearest daughter. We have our
own lives. Both of us need to find
our own space, to explore
the world about us, to extend
our own abilities.
But, like it or not,
we are bound to one another.
It is the lightest of links –
so light that sometimes
we seem to forget it
altogether. But it is stronger than
life itself. One tiny tug will have
me dropping any masterpiece on
which I am engaged –
you are, above everything,
the heartbeat of my life.

We've done well – seen wonders, dreamed dreams. Perhaps we haven't made a circumnavigation of the world, or climbed Everest, or written a best seller. Yet. We've different tastes, different skills, different ambitions. But we like to watch the other live and learn – and to applaud when it's called for. Perhaps we're not everyone's conventional idea of a mother and daughter. Perhaps there's no such thing. But we like each other. We encourage each other. We are friends.

When I am feeling weary
and all the world is dreary
with thin incessant rain,
I think about my daughter,
her brightness and her laughter,
and life comes right again.

Never forget – you're not just special to me.
You're special. And that's that.

I *could* say you were the cleverest,
the most beautiful, the most
perceptive, even-tempered, wise,
considerate daughter in the *entire*
universe. But that wouldn't be right.
I've not *met* all the daughters in the universe.
I can only judge by my
limited acquaintance.
But on *that* basis I say you are the cleverest,
the most beautiful, the most....

THANK YOU!

Thank you for having given me the chance
to make mud pies again, to paddle in the sea,
to sail toy boats, to ride the fairground horses,
to try everything in the children's museum
exhibit – and to stroke all the goats in
the children's zoo. Thank you for an excuse to
make home-made jam and bake birthday cakes.
Thank you for bringing back fun
to all our lives.

Thank you for believing my birthday cakes
were magical, my paintings amazing
and my stories were the best in the world.

Sometimes when I'm feeling particularly
useless you give me sound advice –
which I once gave you.
Thanks for keeping an eye on me, Love.

It is always a surprise to find you have
a daughter as young as yourself.
Thank you, dear, for not thinking I am old.

The best thing you have given me
is your friendship.

YOUR GIFTS TO ME

A child gives us our own first times
all over again.
I have watched marvel
rise in your face, the hushing
of a concert hall as the baton lifts,
the first sight of the sea.
Thank you for reawakening wonder.

Thank you for wilting dandelions,
for twigs of apple blossom, for wet pebbles,
for fluff-covered toffees, for sticky kisses.
Thank you for loving me.
Some daughters give florists' bouquets,
Cartier watches.
Some daughters send shrubs,
and home-made jam. The thing is –
daughters know *exactly* what one needs.

Thank you for newspaper articles you
thought might interest me.
Thank you for the phone call to tell me
of a TV documentary that's just starting.
Thank you for birthday cards that are
exactly right. Thank you for asking me
for recipes. Thank you for giving me advice.
Thank you for letting me into your life.

Thank you for showing me, when I thought
my mothering days were over, that the best days
between us are only just beginning.

There is nothing, absolutely nothing
that can cheer up a dismal evening of
TV repeats and yesterday's leftovers
more successfully than a phone call
from a daughter.

With you away adventuring, the house
seems very flubsy and dull.
My mind half makes plans to go to sea again,
or cross the Sahara in a Land Rover or
some such. But then I catch sight of myself
in the mirror and I realize sadly
that my shinning-up-the-rigging and
brewing-up-in-camp days are over.
You'll just have to do it for me.
Have as much fun and excitement as I did.
Boil the water. Shake the bedding.
Keep your feet in good order.
And write your diary.
My mind and heart are with you.

You will choose your own faith.
Perhaps you will revere a god, a prophet,
a teacher. All I ask is that you show reverence
for every living thing that shares your world.
If you must destroy, destroy only from necessity
and with full knowledge of what you do.
We are indissolubly
linked one with the other.

You have to fight your own battles, Love.
But I'm here in your corner
with the bucket and sponge.

When you were very small
I could kiss most things better.
Or quietly, gently rock you to sleep.
I could mend most things that a kiss
couldn't cure – with glue and tape,
a needle and thread, elastic,
staples, string. I was very good
at replacing dolls' eyeballs –
and arms and legs. And hair.
But now there are things
I cannot stick together, or heal
with a hug.
Grown up matters beyond my skills.
I wish I had some magic
that could make such things come right.
All I can do is be here. Always.

HOPES AND DREAMS

My hope for you is that all your life
you will go on being astonished and delighted
by the world about you.

Of course I dream I could give you all
the places I couldn't take you –
Florence and Venice and Rome, Paris and Prague.
I wish you your own places,
your own adventures, your own loves.

No, Love, I don't dream of wealth
and success for you. Only a job
you like, skills you can perfect,
enthusiasms to lighten your heart, friends
and love in abundance.

Dearest – with all these technical wonders
around us I'm going to wish you something
incredibly old fashioned.
The joy of reading books.
One mind speaking to another across time
and space.

Dear. I hope that when you are very,
very old you can look back and say
"Heavens. That was a *lovely* life."

You have my love – the love that links us.
Take it with you into the world that
I will never know.

MY WISHES FOR YOU

I wish you happy and secure
and comfortable and wise. But not yet.
Get the adventures in first.

How can I wish you anything?
Save that you find what you want to do
and do it. Well.

I wish you the beauty of silence,
the glory of sunlight, the mystery
of darkness, the force of flame,
the power of water, the sweetness of air,
the quiet strength of earth,
the love that lies at the very root of things.
I wish you the wonder of living.

What do I *most* wish for you?
A belief in the fundamental worth of human
kind, and that, my dear, includes yourself.

I wish you love. Romance, yes. But, too, the love
of those who lie together in the darkness,
talking of times past.
The reaching up of children's arms,
the honey-sticky kisses.
The butt of a small cat's head.
A dog's companionable sigh.
The reassuring touch, the lighting up of eyes,
the sound of a key in the lock.

I wish you a daughter just like you.